YOUR KNOWLEDGE HAS VALUE

- We will publish your bachelor's and master's thesis, essays and papers

- Your own eBook and book - sold worldwide in all relevant shops

- Earn money with each sale

Upload your text at www.GRIN.com
and publish for free

Bibliographic information published by the German National Library:

The German National Library lists this publication in the National Bibliography; detailed bibliographic data are available on the Internet at http://dnb.dnb.de .

This book is copyright material and must not be copied, reproduced, transferred, distributed, leased, licensed or publicly performed or used in any way except as specifically permitted in writing by the publishers, as allowed under the terms and conditions under which it was purchased or as strictly permitted by applicable copyright law. Any unauthorized distribution or use of this text may be a direct infringement of the author s and publisher s rights and those responsible may be liable in law accordingly.

Imprint:

Copyright © 2017 GRIN Verlag
Print and binding: Books on Demand GmbH, Norderstedt Germany
ISBN: 9783668632899

This book at GRIN:

https://www.grin.com/document/412438

Oskar Luong

The United Nations Human Rights Council as the Successor to the United Nations Commission on Human Rights

An Analysis of the UN Human Rights Council's Work, Functions and Accountability

GRIN Verlag

GRIN - Your knowledge has value

Since its foundation in 1998, GRIN has specialized in publishing academic texts by students, college teachers and other academics as e-book and printed book. The website www.grin.com is an ideal platform for presenting term papers, final papers, scientific essays, dissertations and specialist books.

Visit us on the internet:

http://www.grin.com/

http://www.facebook.com/grincom

http://www.twitter.com/grin_com

The United Nations Human Rights Council as the successor to the United Nations Commission on Human Rights

I. History

„Recognizing the [...] need to preserve and build on [the] achievements [of the UN Commission on Human Rights] and to *redress its shortcomings*",[1] the UN General Assembly (hereinafter G.A.) established the UN Human Rights Council (hereinafter Council) as the Commission's replacement[2] by resolution 60/251 on 15 March 2006.

After its inception in 1946, the UN Commission on Human Rights (hereinafter Commission) concentrated on codifying international human rights, inter alia, the Universal Declaration of Human Rights.

1) Membership

The Commission consisted of 53 member States from the UN Regional Groups: The seats were apportioned to the African Group (fifteen), the Asian Group (twelve), the Eastern European Group (five), the Latin American and Caribbean Group (eleven) as well as the Western European and Others Group (ten).[3] Some of the Commission's member States were responsible for serious human rights violations, e.g. Libya, Zimbabwe and Sudan.[4] In 2003, the UN Secretary-General Kofi Annan established the High-level Panel on Threats, Challenges and Change that consisted of 16 well-known diplomats, politicians and development experts.[5] The panel evaluated the then existing policies and institutions of the UN that were responsible for

---

[1] General Assembly Resolution 60/251, *Human Rights Council*, A/RES/60/251 (3 April 2006), preamble para. 7.
[2] Proposal made in the Report of the Secretary-General's High-level Panel on Threats, Challenges and Change, *A more secure world: Our shared responsibility*, A/59/565 (2 December 2004), para. 291; Proposals to strengthen the human rights treaty bodies in Kofi Annan, *Report of the UN Secretary-General Kofi Annan in the General Assembly*, A/59/2005 (21 March 2005), paras. 140 – 147.
[3] UN Commission on Human Rights, *Report on the sixty-second session*, E/2006/23, E/CN.4/2006/122 (13-27 March 2006), Economic and Social Council Official Records Supplement No. 3, Annex II, pp. 11 – 15; United Nations Commission on Human Rights, http://www.ohchr.org/EN/HRBodies/CHR/Pages/Membership.aspx (accessed on 7 February 2018).
[4] 'The Shame of the United Nations', *The New York Times* (online), 26 February 2006, http://www.nytimes.com/2006/02/26/opinion/the-shame-of-the-united-nations.html (accessed on 7 February 2018).
[5] Report of the Secretary-General's High-level Panel on Threats, Challenges and Change, *A more secure world: Our shared responsibility*, A/59/565 (2 December 2004), Foreword, p. vii.

dealing with current threats to international peace and security.[6] It recommended the expansion of the membership of the Commission to "universal membership" to "underscore that all [parties] are committed by the [UN] Charter to the promotion of human rights".[7] The members of the UN Economic and Social Council elected the Commission's representatives by simple majority, contrary to the electoral process of the Council that requires all members of the G.A. to vote for individual candidates by a two-thirds majority (at least 96 votes).[8] The members of the Commission could be re-elected at any time, whereas the immediate re-election of the Council's members is only allowed once.[9] There were no criteria for the election of the candidates for the Commission, however, the Council's representatives "shall uphold the highest standards in the promotion and protection of human rights, shall fully cooperate with the Council and be reviewed under the universal periodic review mechanism during their term of membership".[10]

2) Polarisation

The Commission was a platform for mutual recriminations: The African and Asian nations claimed that the western States applied double standards to human rights in developing countries.[11] Although the Commission should address all sorts of human rights violations, discussions about the human rights situation in certain African and Asian countries were often prevented on a proposal from a member State approved by a majority vote ('no-action motion').[12] Consequently, the Commission's recommendations and resolutions mostly dealt with

---

[6] Ibid.
[7] Report of the Secretary-General's High-level Panel on Threats, Challenges and Change, *A more secure world: Our shared responsibility*, A/59/565 (2 December 2004), para. 285.
[8] General Assembly Resolution 60/251, *Human Rights Council*, A/RES/60/251 (3 April 2006), para. 8; Gunnar Theissen, *Mehr als nur ein Namenswechsel. Der neue Menschenrechtsrat der Vereinten Nationen*, Zeitschrift für die Vereinten Nationen und ihre Sonderorganisationen (2006), p. 140.
[9] General Assembly Resolution 60/251, *Human Rights Council*, A/RES/60/251 (3 April 2006), para. 7.
[10] Ibid., para. 9.
[11] Gunnar Theissen, *Mehr als nur ein Namenswechsel. Der neue Menschenrechtsrat der Vereinten Nationen*, Zeitschrift für die Vereinten Nationen und ihre Sonderorganisationen (2006), pp. 138 – 139.
[12] Based on Article 2 of Rule 65 of Rules of Procedure of the Functional Commissions of the Economic and Social Council of the United Nations: E/5975/Rev.1.

States that were too weak to form political alliances with other UN delegations. Ultimately, the meetings of the Commission became a platform for political finger pointing.[13]

As a subsidiary body of the UN Economic and Social Council, the Commission's status was too weak to address human rights violations properly, whereas the Council is the G.A.'s subsidiary organ[14] giving its statements more authority and emphasis within and outside of the UN.

3) Reaction to serious human rights violations

The Commission only held a six-week meeting on an annual basis (with the exception of only four special sessions throughout 60 years), which made it impossible to react adequately to human rights crises reported by the special rapporteurs resulting in its incapability to prosecute serious human rights violations, whereas the Council schedules at least three sessions with a total duration of ten weeks each year and special sessions can be approved by a third of its members.[15] Although the Commission held special sessions regarding the serious human rights crises in the former Yugoslavia (after the breakup in 1992), Rwanda (genocide in 1994), East Timor (crisis following the independence referendum in 1999) and Israel/Palestine (2000), there was only enough time to address other human rights issues during the annual meeting lasting six weeks.

II. The scope of the Council's activities and its main functions

As an intergovernmental organisation composed of 47 member States, the Council promotes universal respect for and protects human rights and fundamental freedoms worldwide, without distinction of any kind.[16] "[T]he membership shall be based on equitable geographical distribution, and seats shall be distributed as follows among regional groups:"[17] Thirteen seats for the group of African States, thirteen seats for the group of Asian States, six seats for the group

---

[13] Kevin Boyle, *New Institutions for Human Rights Protection* (Oxford University Press, 2009), pp. 26 – 27.
[14] General Assembly Resolution 60/251, *Human Rights Council*, A/RES/60/251 (3 April 2006), para. 1.
[15] Ibid., para. 10.
[16] Ibid., para. 2.
[17] Ibid., para. 7.

of Eastern European States, eight seats for the group of Latin American and Caribbean States and seven seats for the group of Western European and other States.[18] By providing education on human rights, technical assistance and capacity building as well as being an international forum for dialogue, the Council addresses and takes action against human rights issues in specific countries by giving not legally binding recommendations to the G.A. regarding the implementation of human rights and the development of public international law to provide a better framework for that.[19] But the Council also develops instruments with legal force (like the protocol introducing a complaints procedure for the Convention on the Rights of the Child) and sets universal standards (like in the guidelines on human rights and private enterprises).[20] Since the Council's inception, over 1400 resolutions have been dealing, inter alia, with topics like democracy, human trafficking, torture, freedom of expression, assembly and association, gender equality and the rule of law.[21] During 26 emergency sessions serious human rights abuses and atrocities in certain countries were condemned, e.g. committed during the "Arab Spring" in 2010 in Libya and Syria or by the terrorist organisation Boko Haram.[22] International Commissions of Inquiry and Fact-Finding missions function as the "eyes and ears of the Council" to investigate war crimes and crimes against humanity, to find evidence and to discover the perpetrators, e.g. in Iraq, South Sudan and recently Myanmar.[23]

Unlike the Commission, the Council has shown that it can deal with human rights issues with a variety of methods, instruments and work closely together with other bodies such as the International Commissions of Inquiry and Fact-Finding missions.

---

[18] Ibid.; See the list of current member States of the Council in: United Nations Human Rights Council, http://www.ohchr.org/EN/HRBodies/HRC/Pages/Membership.aspx (accessed on 6 February 2018).
[19] General Assembly Resolution 60/251, *Human Rights Council*, A/RES/60/251 (3 April 2006), para. 5(a); UN News Centre, http://www.un.org/News/dh/infocus/hr_council/hr_q_and_a.htm (accessed on 6 February 2018).
[20] Permanent Mission of Switzerland to the United Nations Office, *The Human Rights Council – A practical guide* (2005), p. 5.
[21] United Nations, http://www.ohchr.org/Documents/HRBodies/HRCouncil/HRC_briefingnote_En.pdf (version of 30 June 2017, accessed on 6 February 2018).
[22] Ibid.
[23] United Nations Human Rights Office of the High Commissioner, http://www.ohchr.org/Documents/HRBodies/HRCouncil/HRC_English_Final.pdf (accessed on 7 February 2018).

III. Accountability

The Council is a subsidiary organ of the G.A. that reviewed the status of the Council in 2011 (five years after its establishment).[24] Therefore, the Intergovernmental Working Group on the Council Review was established.[25] The Council reports to the G.A. on an annual basis.[26] NGOs like Human Rights Watch assist the Council as well as monitor its activities, make aware of existing human rights issues and if necessary, publicly criticise the member's actions and hold them accountable.[27] Several NGOs called the G.A.'s review of the Council a "deplorable lack of progress" in relation to the protection of human rights, e.g. the torture of prisoners of war in Guantanamo by the US, and the statements "almost an exact replica" compared to the Council's last session in October 2010, especially criticising the speech of the Egyptian Ambassador about his so-called "seven pillars of wisdom" that did not include terms like human rights protection, prevention and responsibility.[28]

Due to the publication of every resolution made by the Council, it can be criticised and held accountable for failures by the public and the media at any time.

IV. Example of how one of the Council's functions works

Among the Council's subsidiary bodies is the Universal Periodic Review mechanism (UPR) which is a peer review system: Every UN member State, including all elected members of the Council, has to submit to a periodic review of its human rights record every four years.[29] The "basis of the review" are the UN Charter, the Universal Declaration of Human Rights, human rights instruments to which a State is party, "voluntary pledges and commitments made by States, including those undertaken when presenting their candidatures for election to the Hu-

---

[24] General Assembly Resolution 60/251, *Human Rights Council*, A/RES/60/251 (3 April 2006), para. 1.
[25] General Assembly Resolution 12/1, *Open-ended intergovernmental working group on the review of the work and functioning of the Human Rights Council*, A/HRC/RES/12/1, para. 1 (12 October 2009).
[26] General Assembly Resolution 60/251, *Human Rights Council*, A/RES/60/251 (3 April 2006), para. 5(j).
[27] Denis Balibouse/Reuters, https://www.hrw.org/topic/united-nations/human-rights-council (published in 2014, accessed on 6 February 2017).
[28] Human Rights Watch, https://www.hrw.org/news/2011/02/09/review-human-rights-council-deplorable-lack-progress (published on 9 February 2011, accessed on 6 February 2018).
[29] General Assembly Resolution 60/251, *Human Rights Council*, A/RES/60/251 (3 April 2006), para. 5(e).

man Rights Council" and international humanitarian law.[30] The human rights performance of all 193 UN member States were placed under scrutiny two times leading to domestic human rights reforms and strengthening justice systems and accountability for violations.[31] This procedure acknowledges the fact that there is no country with clean human rights records and that continuous improvements are necessary for a steady development of promoting and protecting human rights worldwide. The UPR "shall complement and not duplicate the work of treaty bodies".[32] No State can avoid that public attention is being paid to human rights violations, but the current approach aims to be more cooperative than confrontational[33] after learning from the shortcomings of the meetings of the Council's predecessor, the UN Commission on Human Rights.

V. Conclusion

The composition of the membership of the Commission caused many problems for the constructive discussion and an effective decision-making process. The newly introduced requirements regarding the electoral process of the Council's members largely solved these issues. Being a subsidiary organ of the G.A., the Council has a stronger status than the Commission's position as a subsidiary organ of the UN Economic and Social Council. With the help of the UPR, there is no member State whose human rights situation is not examined. Taking all factors into account, the G.A.'s decision to establish the UN Human Rights Council as the successor to the UN Commission on Human Rights was a necessary reform to ensure and enhance international human rights protection.

---

[30] Human Rights Council Resolution 5/1, *Institution-building of the United Nations Human Rights Council*, A/HRC/RES/5/1 (18 June 2007), Annex paras. 1 – 2.
[31] United Nations, http://www.ohchr.org/Documents/HRBodies/HRCouncil/HRC_briefingnote_En.pdf (version of 30 June 2017, accessed on 6 February 2018).
[32] General Assembly Resolution 60/251, *Human Rights Council*, A/RES/60/251 (3 April 2006), para. 5(e).
[33] Ian Brownlie and Guy S. Goodwin-Gill, *Brownlie's Documents on Human Rights* (Oxford University Press, 6th edition 2010), p. 14.

Bibliography

UN Documents/International Materials

- Annan, Kofi, Report of the UN Secretary-General Kofi Annan in the General Assembly, A/59/2005 (21 March 2005)
- General Assembly Resolution 12/1, Open-ended intergovernmental working group on the review of the work and functioning of the Human Rights Council, A/HRC/RES/12/1 (12 October 2009)
- General Assembly Resolution 60/251, Human Rights Council, A/RES/60/251 (3 April 2006)
- Report of the Secretary-General's High-level Panel on Threats, Challenges and Change, A more secure world: Our shared responsibility, A/59/565 (2 December 2004)
- Rules of Procedure of the Functional Commissions of the Economic and Social Council of the United Nations, E/5975/Rev.1
- United Nations Human Rights Office of the High Commissioner, Commissions of Inquiry and Fact-Finding missions on International Human Rights and Humanitarian Law – Guidance and Practice (2015), available from http://www.ohchr.org/Documents/Publications/CoI_Guidance_and_Practice.pdf (accessed on 7 February 2018)

Books/Articles

- Boyle, Kevin, New Institutions for Human Rights Protection, Oxford University Press, (2009)
- Brownlie, Ian and Goodwin-Gill, Guy S., Brownlie's Documents on Human Rights, Oxford University Press, 6th edition (2010)
- Permanent Mission of Switzerland to the United Nations Office, The Human Rights Council – A practical guide (2015), available from https://www.eda.admin.ch/content/dam/eda/en/documents/publications/Internationale Organisationen/Uno/Human-rights-Council-practical-guide_en (accessed on 7 February 2018)
- The New York Times (online), The Shame of the United Nations (26 February 2006), http://www.nytimes.com/2006/02/26/opinion/the-shame-of-the-united-nations.html (accessed on 7 February 2018).
- Theissen, Gunnar, 'Mehr als nur ein Namenswechsel. Der neue Menschenrechtsrat der Vereinten Nationen', Zeitschrift für die Vereinten Nationen und ihre Sonderorganisationen, Heft 4 (2006)

Websites

- Denis Balibouse/Reuters, https://www.hrw.org/topic/united-nations/human-rights-council (published in 2014, accessed on 6 February 2017).
- Human Rights Watch, https://www.hrw.org/news/2011/02/09/review-human-rights-council-deplorable-lack-progress (published on 9 February 2011, accessed on 6 February 2018)

- UN News Centre, http://www.un.org/News/dh/infocus/hr_council/hr_q_and_a.htm (accessed on 6 February 2018)
- United Nations Commission on Human Rights, http://www.ohchr.org/EN/HRBodies/CHR/Pages/Membership.aspx (accessed on 7 February 2018)
- United Nations Human Rights Office of the High Commissioner, http://www.ohchr.org/Documents/HRBodies/HRCouncil/HRC_English_Final.pdf (accessed on 7 February 2018)
- United Nations, http://www.ohchr.org/Documents/HRBodies/HRCouncil/HRC_briefingnote_En.pdf (version of 30 June 2017, accessed on 6 February 2018)

YOUR KNOWLEDGE HAS VALUE

- We will publish your bachelor's and master's thesis, essays and papers

- Your own eBook and book - sold worldwide in all relevant shops

- Earn money with each sale

Upload your text at www.GRIN.com
and publish for free